Dear Mom...

You mean so very much to me and there is not a day that goes by that I don't think of you and wish that we could be closer. Happy Mother's Day because Your my Mom and I love You more everyday

Love,
Your daughter, Heather Renae

Long may you live, happy may you be;
Loved by all, but best by me.

5/9/99

Grateful appreciation is expressed to
Rhonda Hogan for her research assistance.

Illustrations copryighted ©1999 by Judy Buswell
and used by permission.
Cover/interior design by Koechel Peterson & Associates.

Dear Mom

A BOOK OF

LOVING

THOUGHTS

Compiled by
Caroline Brownlow

Illustrated by
Judy Buswell

Brownlow

Just One Touch

Everybody knows that a good mother gives her children a feeling of trust and stability. She is their earth. She is the one they can count on for the things that matter most of all. She is their food and their bed and the extra blanket when it grows cold in the night; she is their warmth and their health and their shelter; she is the one they want to be near when they cry. She is the only person in the whole world or in a whole lifetime who can be these things to her children. There is no substitute for her. Somehow even her clothes feel different to her children's hands from anybody else's clothes. Only to touch her skirt or her sleeve makes a troubled child feel better.

KATHERINE BUTLER HATHAWAY

*M*other holds her children's hands for a while,
their hearts forever.

ANONYMOUS

*T*he mother love is like God's love;
He loves us not because we are lovable,
but because it is His nature to love,
and because we are His children.

EARL RINEY

*C*hildren aren't ever sure what they want,
but that's not the point—it's that they want it NOW.

E. COSTELLO

I find life an exciting business,
and most exciting when it is lived for others.

HELEN KELLER

Selfless Love

Mothers are selfless people. They spend most of their lives caring for others, trying to meet the needs of their children and family. As a result, they spend their days doing countless loads of laundry, driving miles of errands, baking cookies at midnight, spending hours in the kitchen preparing our favorite meals, washing worlds of dirty dishes, cleaning up all the messes we made, being a gracious hostess for innumerable slumber parties, listening patiently to the pangs of a first love, advising gently the growth of a new adult, watching hopefully as her children take wing. A mother does all this and more without even a ripple of applause. She does it all because it is her nature to love. The final satisfaction, however, comes when she sees her children carrying on the legacy of love that she has so carefully passed down, and she smiles.

RHONDA S. HOGAN

Children despise their parents until the age of forty, when they suddenly become just like them, thus preserving the system.

QUENTIN CREWE

The woman who creates and sustains a home and under whose hands children grow up to be strong and pure men and women, is a creator second only to God.

HELEN HUNT JACKSON

Home–Where Hearts Are Sure

Home is the one place in all this world where hearts are sure of each other. It is the place of confidence. It is the place where we tear off that mask of guarded and suspicious coldness which the world forces us to wear in self-defense, and where we pour out the unreserved communications of full and confiding hearts. It is the spot where expressions of tenderness gush out without any sensation of awkwardness and without any dread of ridicule.

It is quite simply a place of love.

FREDERICK W. ROBERTSON

For the mother is and must be,
whether she knows it or not, the greatest,
strongest and most lasting teacher her children have.

HANNAH WHITALL SMITH

What do girls do
who haven't any mothers
to help them through their troubles?

LOUISA MAY ALCOTT

All mothers are physically handicapped.
They have only two hands.

ANONYMOUS

Love is not blind; love sees a great deal more
than the actual. Love sees the ideal, the potential in us.

OSWALD CHAMBERS

One mother achieves more than a hundred teachers.

JEWISH PROVERB

A Mother's Faith

I believe in the eternal importance of the home
as the fundamental institution of society.
I believe in the immeasurable possibilities of every boy and girl.
I believe in the imagination, the trust, the hopes and the ideals
which dwell in the hearts of all children.
I believe in the beauty of nature, of art, of books, and of friendship.
I believe in the satisfactions of duty.
I believe in the little homely joys of everyday life.
I believe in the goodness of the great design which lies
behind our complex world.
I believe in the safety and peace which surround us all
through the overbrooding love of God.

OZORA DAVIS

*M*aking the decision to have a child—
it's momentous. It is to decide forever
to have your heart go walking
around outside your body.

ELIZABETH STONE

*I*f it was going to be easy to rear children,
it never would have started
with something called "labor."

ANONYMOUS

*R*ejecting things because they are old-fashioned
would rule out the sun and the
moon—and a mother's love.

ANONYMOUS

*S*pare the rod and spoil the child is true.
But beside the rod, keep an apple to give him,
when he has done well.

MARTIN LUTHER

*J*ust when a mother thinks her work is done,
she becomes a grandmother.

CAROLINE BROWNLOW

Mother Won't Let Me

A policeman noticed a boy with a lot of stuff packed
on his back riding a tricycle around and around the block.
Finally he asked him where he was going.

"I'm running away from home," the boy said.

The policeman then asked him, "Why do you keep going
around and around the block?"

The boy answered,

"My mother won't let me cross the street."

*M*any make the household
but only one the home.

JAMES RUSSELL LOWELL

*A*ffection is resposible fot nine-tenths
of whatever solid and durable happiness
there is in our natural lives.

C. S. LEWIS

*M*other is the name for God
on the lips and hearts of little children.

WILLIAM MAKEPEACE THACKERAY

*W*hen a mother forgives,
she kisses the offense
into everlasting forgiveness.

HENRY WARD BEECHER

I Love You, Mom

I love you not only for what you are, but for what I am when
I am with you. I love you not only for what you have made of
yourself, but for what you are making of me.
I love you for the part of me that you bring out.

I love you for putting your hand into my heaped-up heart, and
passing over all the foolish and frivolous and weak things which
you cannot help dimly seeing there, and for drawing out into
the light all the beautiful, radiant belongings,
that no one else had looked quite far enough to find.

I love you for ignoring the possibilities of the fool and weakling
in me, and for laying firm hold on the possibilities of good in
me. I love you for closing your eyes to the discords in me,
and for adding to the music in me by worshipful listening.

I love you because you have done more than any creed could
have done to make me good, and more than any fate could have
done to make me happy. You have done it just by being yourself.
Perhaps that is what being a mom means after all.

These are the children
God has given me.
God has been good to me.

GENESIS 33:5

To become a mother
is not hard.
To be a mother is.

RHONDA S. HOGAN

A World of
Beautiful Thoughts

For when you looked into my mother's

eyes you knew, as if He had told you,

why God sent her into the world—

it was to open the minds of all who looked,

to beautiful thoughts.

SIR JAMES M. BARRIE

A mother is someone who dreams for you,
but then lets you chase the dreams you have
for yourself and loves you just the same.

ANONYMOUS

*L*ove is a fruit in season at all times,
and within reach of every hand.
Anyone may gather it and no limit is set.

MOTHER TERESA

*P*eople who say they sleep like a baby
usually don't have one.

LEO J. BURKE

*O*ur children are likely
to live up to what we believe of them.

LADY BIRD JOHNSON

On Earth
There Is No Other

There is but one and only one,

Whose love will fail you never.

One who lives from sun to sun,

With constant fond endeavor.

There is but one and only one,

On earth there is no other.

In heaven a noble work was done,

When God gave us a Mother.

A Mother's Prayer

Lord, give me patience when wee hands

Tug at me with their small demands.

Give me gentle and smiling eyes;

Keep my lips from hasty replies.

Let not weariness, confusion, or noise

Obscure my vision of life's fleeting joys.

So, when in years to come, my house is still—

No bitter memories its rooms may fill.

*B*eing a mother enables one to influence the future.

JANE SELLMAN

*H*er children arise and call her blessed.

PROVERBS 31:28

*M*other's love grows by giving.

CHARLES LAMB

*C*hildren have neither past nor future;
they enjoy the present, which very few of us do.

LABRUYERE

*C*hildren do not know
how much their parents love them,
and they never will until
they have children of their own.

COOKE